REFLECTIONS
ON
CATS

Edited by
Margaret Neylon

Attic Press
Dublin

First published in 1993 by
Attic Press,
4 Upper Mount Street
Dublin 2

British Library Cataloguing in Publication Data
A catalogue record for this book is available from the British Library.

ISBN 1-85594-064-7

Cover Design: Katharine White
Origination: Attic Press
Printing: Leinster Leader Print, Kildare

Attic Reflections Series

During the past few years we have seen an explosion of interest in the area generally referred to as New Age. This can be seen in the enormous growth in the number of people taking an alternative approach to all aspects of living in the modern world.

The search for new alternatives reaches into the area of spirituality and personal development, with many seeking answers to questions of personal growth outside the more traditional methods.

In response to this need Attic Press launched the **ATTIC REFLECTIONS SERIES**.

We continue to add to this series with relevant and resourceful Reflections.

Beautifully presented and illustrated, these books will be ones you will find yourself returning to again and again.

Other titles in the
Attic Reflections Series

DEDICATION

In fond memory of Leo

MARGARET NEYLON lives in Dublin where she is Creative Director of an advertising agency. A short story writer and playwright, much of her work has been produced on radio. She is also author of *Pathways: A Source Book of Life Options* (Attic Press, 1991) and editor of *Wit and Wisdom* (Attic Press, 1992)

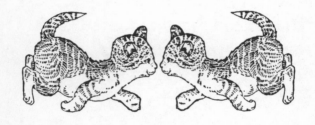

... If they are content, their contentment is absolute; and our jaded and wearied spirits find natural relief in the sight of creatures whose little cups of happiness can so easily be filled to the brim.

Agnes Repplier

Bless their little pointed faces
and their big, loyal, loving hearts.
If a cat did not put a firm paw
down now and then
How could her human remain
possessed.

Winifred Carriere

You see the beauty of the world
Through eyes of unalloyed content,
And in my study chair upcurled,
Move me to pensive wonderment.

                                            Anon

If there is one spot of sun spilling onto the floor, a cat will find it and soak it up.

Joan Asper McIntosh

A cat improves the garden wall in sunshine,
and the hearth in foul weather ...
Judith Merkle Riley

Cats ... never strike a pose that isn't photogenic.

Lillian Jackson Braun

Cats speak to poets in their natural tongue, and something profound and untamed in us answers.

                                        Jean Burden

No one can have experienced to the fullest the true sense of achievement and satisfaction who has never pursued and successfully caught her tail.

Rosalind Welcher

When I'm discouraged, she's
empathy incarnate, purring and
rubbing to telegraph her dismay ...

Catheryn Jakobson

You can't look at a sleeping cat and be tense.

Jane Pauley

How many times have I rested tired eyes on her graceful little body, curled up in a ball and wrapped round with her tail like a parcel ...

Agnes Repplier

I think it would be great to be a cat!
You come and go as you please.
People always feed and pet you.
They don't expect much of you. You
can play with them, and when
you've had enough, you go away.
You can pick and choose who you
want to be around. You can't ask for
more than that.

Patricia McPherson

... it is better, under certain circumstances to be a cat than to be a duchess ... No duchess of the realm ever had more faithful retainers or half so abject subjects.

Helen M. Winslow

If a fish is the movement of water embodied,
given shape,
then a cat is a diagram and pattern
of subtle air.

Doris Lessing

At night, in the dark, all cats are grey.

Adage

A charm of cats is that they seem to live in a world of their own, just as much as if it were a real dimension of space.

Harriet Prescott Spofford

I saw the most beautiful Cat today. It was sitting by the side of the road, its two front feet neatly and graciously together. Then it gravely swished around its tail to completely and snugly encircle itself. It was so fit and beautifully neat, that gesture, and so self-satisfied — so complacent.

Anne Morrow Lindbergh

... *When she walked ... she stretched out long and thin like a little tiger, and held her head high to look over the grass as if she were threading the jungle.*

Swah One Jewett

It doesn't do to be sentimental about cats, the best ones don't respect you for it ...

Susan Howatch

Some pussies' coats are yellow;
Some amber streaked with dark,
No member of the feline race
But has a special mark.

This one has feet with hoarfrost
tipped;
That one has tail that curls;
Another's inky hide is striped;
Another decked with pearls.

Anon

There are no ordinary cats.

Colette

It is impossible for a lover of cats to banish these alert, gentle, and discriminating little friends, who give us just enough of their regard and complaisance to make us hunger for more.

Agnes Repplier

To understand a cat, you must realise that she has her own gifts, her own viewpoint, even her own morality.

Lillian Jackson Braun

She lives in the half-light in secret places, free and alone — this mysterious little-great being whom her mistress calls 'my cat'.

Margaret Benson

The cat, like the genius, draws into itself as into a shell except in the atmosphere of congeniality, and this is the secret of its remarkable and elusive personality.

Ida M. Mellen

The cat is mighty dignified until the dog comes by.

North American folk saying

No, heaven will not ever heaven be unless my cats are there to welcome me.

Epitaph in a pet cemetery

My little grandson is a darling, but
he can never take the place of my
cats.

Anon

The cat was a creature of absolute convictions, and her faith in her deductions never varied.

Mary E. Wilkins Freeman

There are people who reshape the world by force or argument, but the cat just lies there, dozing, and the world quietly reshapes itself to suit her comfort and convenience.

Ivy Dodd

At dinner time she would sit in a corner, concentrating,
and suddenly they would say, 'time to feed the cat', as if it were their own idea.

Lillian Jackson Braun

No self-respecting cat wants to be an artist's model.

Gina Elgin

Sometimes the veil between human and animal intelligence wears very thin — then one experiences the supreme thrill of keeping a cat, or perhaps allowing oneself to be owned by a cat.

Catherine Manley

A dog, I have always said, is prose; a cat is a poem.

Jean Burden

There is nothing in the animal world, to my mind, more delightful than grown cats at play.
They are so swift and light and graceful, so subtle and designing, and yet so richly comic.

Monica Edwards

The best exercise for a cat is another cat.

Jo Loeb

A kitten is the most irresistible comedian in the world. Its wide-open eyes gleam with wonder and mirth. It darts madly at nothing at all, and then, as though suddenly checked in the pursuit, prances sideways on its hind legs with ridiculous agility and zeal.

Agnes Repplier

He shut his eyes while Saha (the cat)
kept vigil, watching all the invisible
signs that hover over sleeping human
beings when the light is put out.

Colette

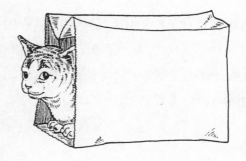

Women, poets and especially artists, like cats; delicate natures only can realise their sensitive nervous systems.

Helen M. Winslow

A kitten is a very special little creature and when you decide to take one into your home you must be prepared to accept full responsibility for its care and welfare. Above all, you will need to provide a great deal of love ... however much you give will be repaid with interest.

Angela Sayer

Purring would seem to be, in her case, an automatic safety-valve device for dealing with happiness overflow.

Monica Edwards

I wish you could see the two cats drowsing side by side in a Victorian nursing chair, their paws, their ears, their tails complementally adjusted, their blue eyes blinking open on a single thought of when I shall remember it's their supper-time. They might have been composed by Bach for two flutes.

> Sylvia Townsend Warner

In a cat's eyes
All things belong to cats.

English proverb

To please herself only the cat purrs.

                    Irish proverb

For push of nose, for perseverance,
there is nothing to beat a cat.

Emily Carr

No matter how tired or wretched I am, a pussy-cat sitting in a doorway can divert my mind.

Mary E. Wilkins Freeman

The cat is, above all things, a dramatist.

Margaret Benson

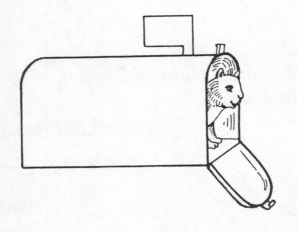

Honest as the cat when the meat is out of reach.

English proverb

Cats have a contempt of speech.
Why should they talk when they can
communicate without words?

Lillian Jackson Braun

Cats love one so much — more than they will allow. But they have so much wisdom they keep it to themselves?

Mary E. Wilkins Freeman

He calls 'meat, meat!'
All down the street,
And dogs 'bow-wow',
And cats 'mi-ow',
While kittens sly
Come purring by'
As if to say —
'Do serve us, pray,
The first of all,
For we're so small.'
The man throws bits
of meat to kits,
And cats, and dogs;
Then on he jogs,
And down the street
Still cries 'meat, meat!!'

Anon

I have just been given a very
engaging Persian kitten.
And her opinion is that I have been
given to her.

Evelyn Underhill

*I have lost friends, some by death —
others by their sheer inability to cross
the street.*

Virginia Woolf

A kitten is more amusing than half the people one is obliged to live with.

Lady Sydney Morgan

Perhaps a child, like a cat, is so much inside herself that she does not see herself in the mirror.

Anaïs Nin

A cat can look at a king.
And a tourist can look at anything.

Eleanor Early

All cats love fish, but fear to wet their paws.

Anon

No animal is so great an enemy to all constraint as the cat.

Brewer's Dictionary of Phrase & Fable

A mouse under the paw of a cat lives
But by sufferance and at the cat's
pleasure only.

Anon

If a cat has decided to love you there's not a great deal you can do about it.

Katrina Smythe

She has as many lives as a cat, and a cat's ability to land on her feet.

Edith Howie

There's more ways of killing a cat than choking it to death with butter.

Mary Lasswell

She was looking around the dinner table with that cat-swallowed-the-canary smile.

Virginia Rath

Cats understand much more than we will ever know.

                              Grace McHattie

Níl áit a'chait sa luaith aige.

He's not allowed even the cat's place by the fire.

Irish Proverb

If your cat presents you with a dead mouse or bird, don't shriek in terror or shout at her. She is bringing you a gift — her contribution to your social group's foodstore. Thank her ... She'll usually be happy to take it away, she was only offering it to you out of politeness anyway.

Grace Mc Hattie

She also occasionally allowed visiting cats who belonged to really good friends, although the air of injured betrayal with which her own cat, the proud and independent-minded Midnight, greeted these intrusions, was hard to bear ... in cat terms he might be right — it was the ultimate betrayal to allow another cat on his territory.

Antonia Fraser

A cat condenses.
She pulls in her tail to go under
bridges.

Rosalie Moore

The dog will come when he is called,
The cat will walk away.

Adelaide O'Keeffee

A mouse in the claws of a cat has no time for squeaking.

> *Armenian Proverb*

The cat who wears gloves will catch no mice.

Russian Proverb

What do cats think about? Nothing the human mind can conceive or vocabulary express. Strange considerations, occult intimations are in the eyes of my little cat.

Marguerite Steen

A cat is a friendly hot water bottle at night, an alarm clock with a wet tongue.

Phillida Law

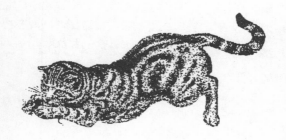

The cat is a loner, the tiger of the housing estate.

Joanne Lorimer

Of all the cats who have owned me
there has never been any like my
white little kitten, for sweetness,
intelligence and affection.

Marguerite Steen

A cat is a lion in a jungle of small bushes.

Indian Proverb

When everyone else is just ready to go out,
The cat is just ready to come in.

Rosalie Moore

A dog will often steal a bone
But conscience lets him not alone
And by his tail his guilt is known.
But cats consider theft a game
And, whosoever you may blame,
Refuse the slightest sign of shame.

Anon

One small cat changes coming home
to an empty house to coming home.

Lucy Wheeler

What is sport for the cat is death for the mouse.

Russian Proverb

You can feel an awful fool standing at the bottom of the garden yelling 'Pussy! Pussy! Pussy!' across a totally deserted meadow. Especially when you realise that Pussy, Pussy, Pussy is watching you, with benign interest, from the shelter of the garden shed.

Marcia Fischer

If you have a cat you need a remote control to your TV. And a butler. There's no huff like the huff of a cat who's chosen his knee for the evening and finds himself forcibly evicted.

Denise Hawkins

Only cat lovers know the luxury of fur-coated, musical hot water bottles that never go cold.

Susanne Millen

If the cat winketh, rain shall fall.

Proverb

Wherever the cat of the house is black,
The lassies of lovers will have no lack.

Adage

A lovely thing it is to own one's first kitten - soft and furry, curled comfortably before one's fireplace.

Catherine Manley

A cat pent up becomes a lion.

Proverb

Curiosity killed the cat.
Satisfaction brought it back.

Proverb

Noah sailing o'er the seas
Ran high and dry on Ararat
His dog then made a spring and took
The tail from off a pussycat.
Puss through the window quick did
fly
And bravely through the water
swam,
Nor even stopped till high and dry
She landed, on the Isle of Man.
This tailless puss earned Mona's
thanks
And ever after was called Manx.

Unknown

A lame cat is better than a swift horse when rats are about.

Adage

A farmer tossed kittens into a river to drown them and a tree on the riverbank, hearing the mother cat's anguish, reached into the water so the kittens could climb to safety on the bank. Ever after, each Spring this tree grows furry buds in memory of this act. We now call this tree the Pussy Willow.

Polish legend

Beware the tiger that lurks in every cat.

Proverb

I can say with sincerity that I like cats. A cat is an animal which has more human feelings than almost any other.

Emily Bronte

To be a cat lover is one thing, to be a show enthusiast another, and the consensus of opinion is that the former is very commendable, while the latter is a little suspect.

Mary Eustace

Our perfect companions never have fewer than four feet.

Colette

Siamese cats cannot be blamed if they are thieves; after all, they have no moral code. They are so sharp-witted and sensitive to smell that they will soon nose out the good things in life.

Mary Eustace

Too old a cat to be fooled by a kitten.

Adage

When in ripe years she left us
Her last feeble breath was a purr,
And if the doors of Heaven are
closed to such as her,
I see no better hope for you and me.

Caroline Marriage

A cat came fiddling out of a barn
With a pair of bagpipes under her
arm.
She could sing nothing but fiddle-
cum-fee
The mouse has married the bumble-
bee!
Pipe cat, dance mouse,
We'll have a wedding at our good
house.

Old rhyme

Who shall tell the lady's grief
When her cat was past relief?
Who shall number the hot tears
Shed o'er her, belov'd for years?
Who shall say the dark dismay
Which her dying caused today?

Christina Rossetti

A cat that lives with a good family is used to being talked to all the time.

Lettice Cooper

A black cat dropped soundlessly from a high wall, like a spoonful of dark treacle, and melted under a gate.

Elizabeth Lemarchand

House without hound, cat or child is a house without love or affection.

Adage

Cats are curious creatures. If a door is opened wide they often have no desire to go out or come in. But open it a crack, so they can't see right through it and, convinced they are missing something, they will go through.

Moyra Bremner

People enrich their lives in many ways ... we all have our conception of that which gives us pleasure and gladdens our hearts ... Apart from a dog here and there, with me ... it's cats.

Betty Lester

Su sometimes goes on safari. Luckily her hosts are cat lovers and do not take fright when they find a stranger in their bed.

May Eustace

The three fortunes of a cat: the cook's forgetfulness, walking without a sound, and keen sight in the dark.

Adage

Su's kittens are like herself, adventurous and gay. Once they spent a whole afternoon 'killing' a pillow. This resembled a scene from Swan Lake, with leaping forms floating in the air, covered with down and feathers ... Another time they curled up in a cake-tin like a beautiful risen madeira.

May Eustace

I have heard of a brandy-drinking cat. Poor puss was taken ill and milk and brandy tried. It rallied. When afterwards plain milk was offered it, it declined till brandy was added.

Christina Rossetti

Be soft. Be cool. Be mysterious.
Know all the sunny places.

Suzy Becker

A friend tells me of a cat who, when its mistress lay dying, laid at her door first a mouse and then a bird to tempt her appetite.

Christina Rossetti

There is something about cats that makes people either want to be their undying slave, or dislike them intensely; indifference is rare.

Dorothy Silkstone Richards

All I need to know I learned from my cat.

Suzy Becker

It is said that the Siamese has a squint because of the long time it spent gazing at the treasure it guarded from thieves in the Buddhist temples.

Eastern legend

Two cats are always better than one, for the feline has a mysterious mathematical formula all its own in which two cats together seem able to provide more than double the happiness afforded its owner by one cat.

Angela Sayer

I live with my few friends and my many cats.

Leonor Fini

... I should say that I have had cats all my life and am glad to say that none of them has ever sprayed, soiled in the headphones of the hi-fi or eaten my underwear.

Joyce Hayes

These (Siamese) cats are extroverts and extremely agile, never doing anything by halves, which means that an owner must be prepared for a pet that will release pent-up energy by climbing the curtains and, metaphorically, swinging from the chandelier.

Katherine Tottenham

*You have only to observe a cat —
any cat — for a short while to see
what a perfect machine it is for
hunting.*

Anna Sproule

... Cat/atonic n: healing exhilaration achieved through the companionship of Felicitous Felines.

Mary Daly & Jane Caputi

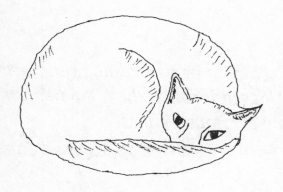

When rain is coming cats stop play
and compose themselves.

Adage

Cats do not become ghosts as they live their nine lives fully upon this earth during one lifetime.

Gaelic Belief

Be hard to leave ... Be easy to come home to.

Suzy Becker

If a black cat comes into your house on Christmas night you will have great luck for a full year.

Irish legend

At 10 o'clock sharp every night Seeley climbed onto my lap, tapped me on the cheek with a soft but urgent paw, and when she'd got my attention, fixed me with a look that meant Milk. In the kitchen. Now.

Doreen Tovey

Cats in Ancient Egypt enjoyed a long life, a natural death and a burial with the honours of the State.

Egyptian lore

When a cat turns its back to the fire
it portends rain.

Irish legend

Mac Cavity of Hampstead ... seems to think he is a dog. He sits when told, comes when I call, opens doors with his paws, answers when spoken to and, being a polite, well-brought up cat, always shuts the doors after himself.

Nina Epton

The older and more hairless the cat, the more fortune it will bring the household.

Asian legend

The Chinese exchanged pure silk for cats. In addition to destroying rodents they were considered to symbolise peace, fortune and family serenity.

Eastern lore

She flew down the garden with the long rippling strides of a tiger ... and took the wall with the graceful leap of a front runner at the Grand National.

Sheila Whitelaw

Cats have a built-in time mechanism and they are often more reliable — and gentle — than alarm clocks ...
                                    Nina Epton

Communication is a two-way street.
If you can establish this you are in
for some extraordinary and most
rewarding experiences. (Remember
that the cat is a provident animal ...
you will get exactly what you give,
just as you do in your daily
relationships with family, friends
and business associates.)

Roseanne Amberson

She tipped her out and she fell head first, somersaulting with a neat twist of her body. It was a normal feline four-point landing after an awkward take-off.

Sheila Whitelaw

The cat is her best adviser.

Irish legend

Often some folk think I'm bats
'Cos I spend so much time with cats
But feline company I favour
When compared to some behaviour.
They've more than beauty of the
face,
They've character and so much grace.
So all in all I think to me
The cat is perfect company.

                              Margaret Neylon

Cats are contradictions:
Tooth and claw.

Phoebe Hesketh

Ginger of County Down, is discouraged from slipping upstairs to lie on a bed. If her mistress sees her setting off up the stairs she calls 'Now, Ginger', and Ginger meekly turns and comes down again. If she calls 'Come to the table, everyone', Ginger is the only one to rush to a chair!

Nina Epton

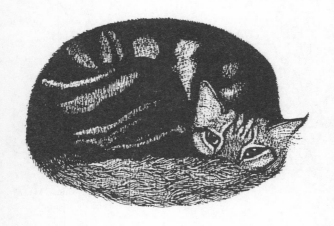

Two wide eyes looked up at her with a touching dignity, without a trace of pleading. They were haunting eyes, a pale amber with a hint of green depths ... The woman and the cat looked at each other and it was something at first sight; something neither could define.

Sheila Whitelaw

Keyword Index

Author Index